CRISIS

VICTORY

BY DR. HAL BRADLEY

Crisis Victory

By Dr. Hal Bradley

Published by Beverly Hills Publishing

468 Camden Drive

Beverly Hills, CA 90210

www.beverlyhillspublishing.com

Copyright © 2020 Beverly Hills Publishing Firm, Beverly Hills, California. All rights reserved.

ISBN: 978-1-7360900-0-8

In no way is it legal to reproduce, duplicate, or transmit any part of this document in either electronic means or in printed format. Recording of this publication is strictly prohibited and any storage of this document is not allowed unless with written permission from the publisher. All rights reserved.

The information provided herein is stated to be truthful and consistent, in that any liability, in terms of inattention or otherwise, by any usage or abuse of any policies, processes, or directions contained within is the solitary and utter responsibility of the recipient reader. Under no circumstances will any legal responsibility or blame be held against the publisher for any reparation, damages, or monetary loss due to the information herein, either directly or indirectly. Respective authors own all copyrights not held by the publisher. The information herein is offered for informational purposes solely and is universal, as so. The presentation of the information is without contract or any type of guarantee assurance.

The trademarks that are used are without any consent, and the publication of the trademark is without permission or backing by the trademark owner. All trademarks and brands within this book are for clarifying ¬purposes only and are the owned by the owners themselves, not affiliated with this document

---

The information and descriptions presented in this book and in the Crisis Victory newsletters and website are intended for adults, age 18 and over, and are solely for informational and educational purposes. Dr. Hal Bradley does not give legal, psychological, or financial advice. Before beginning any new business or personal development routine, or if you have specific legal, psychological, or medical concerns, a medical, financial, legal, or other professional should be consulted.

Any reproduction, republication, or other distribution of this work, including, without limitation, the duplication, copying, scanning, uploading, and making available via the internet or any other means, without the express permission of the publisher is illegal and punishable by law, and the knowing acquisition of an unauthorized reproduction of this work may subject the acquirer to liability. Please purchase only authorized electronic or print editions of this work and do not participate in or encourage electronic piracy of copyrighted materials. Your support of the author's rights is appreciated.

This document is geared towards providing exact and reliable information with regards to the topic and issue covered. The publication is sold with the idea that the publisher is not required to render accounting, officially permitted, or otherwise, qualified services. If advice is necessary, legal or professional, a practiced individual in the profession should be ordered.

– From a Declaration of Principles which was accepted and approved equally by a Committee of the American Bar Association and a Committee of Publishers and Associations.

This book is dedicated to
Victor Mojica & US Special Agent Mark Selby,
former SAC of the Miami Dade U.S. Customs office.

You both were in the right place
at the right time.

Thank you.

I love you both.

Contents

Introduction	7
Chapter 1 Expect to Survive	25
Chapter 2 Finding Resources to Survive in a New Environment	43
Chapter 3 Retrain Your Thinking	53
Chapter 4 Implementation	63
Chapter 5 Acquiring Basic Needs	77
Chapter 6 Communication	89
Chapter 7 Unlocking Meditation	99
Chapter 8 Moving into the New	109

Introduction

A *Fictionalized and Fact-Based Story of the Life of Dr. Hal Bradley, D.D.*

My story begins in 1969. I was a 15-year-old lad from a small city called Edmonds, Washington, and I had just been suspended for a semester as a sophomore for getting caught smoking a cigarette in the bathroom with a couple of friends. My single mother, with three children at home and a fourth serving in Vietnam in the 2nd Marine Division, was raising us alone. She worked at a dry cleaner in downtown Edmonds to support us.

My mother had a friend who owned a small, 11 percent interest in the "Anaconda de Mexico" Mining Company in Durango, Mexico. They offered to send me down to work in the mining camps, rather than sit at home for a semester and possibly get into more trouble. So, I packed my things, and moved down to Mexico for over a year.

No one could have known that this decision would forever alter the path of my life.

My transportation to the mine came in the form of a black-and-white spotted burro. I remember learning the trails in those mountains, and that exploration led me to Indian encampments. These were areas established for cultivating marijuana and working the poppy fields. As time went on, I became friends with the growers and harvesters. I lived in Gualterio, and spent my days working deep underground.

I recall regularly seeing upwards of 40 or more burros loaded with marijuana wrapped in burlap being led down the trails to dump trucks waiting in the canyon below. There, they would be loaded and driven away to camps where they would be broken down and formed into kilos. I remember seeing the old and young alike out in those poppy fields, with their cutting blades and a pallet collecting the sap. And when their pallets were filled with the gum from the poppies, they would take their harvest into an adobe shack and come back out to continue picking.

About a year later, I got word that my brother had been wounded in action in Vietnam and was being flown to Bremerton Naval Hospital, across the bay from Seattle. It was at this point that I returned to the United States. I was 16 years old.

After visiting my brother in the hospital, I decided to join the Army myself, and serve as he had in defense of our country. I attended Edmonds Community College and earned my GED. On my 17th birthday I took my oath to serve, and shipped to Fort Knox, Kentucky, for basic training. From there I moved to a special training site at Fort Polk, Louisiana, known as "Tigerland." Due to the intensity and brutality of the training we endured, Tigerland was shut down permanently shortly after I graduated. I left there for Fort Benning, Georgia, for paratrooper school and, after graduation, was shipped to the 8th Infantry Division in Mainz, Germany. By then, I was an experienced 17-year-old. I had already lived through so much.

On March 14, 1974, I was discharged from the U.S. Army and moved to Sacramento, California, where my family had relocated. Using my G.I Bill, I enrolled at Sacramento City College. That winter, during a school break, I made the fateful decision to visit a friend in Gualterio, Durango, Mexico.

When I pulled into the dusty village in my rented Jeep, everyone I had ever known and worked with rushed outside to see me. There was such innocent love and compassion shown to me there, and that was part of the beauty of these people I had missed so very much. There wasn't a home in Gualterio where I wasn't welcome. The villagers threw a feast for me at the pond where I used to bathe and where I watched the women wash their clothing. I had missed this simple life.

My friend who I had come to see, Reuben, talked to me about coming back down to the village later with a larger vehicle – one they could use to hide marijuana and later transport kilos to sell stateside. I agreed, and some months later I made my first run. It was an intense experience, but I loved it. By the time I made it across the border and unloaded the contraband, I had made $80,000, just like that! I drove down again and gave Reuben $20,000, which was more money than he had made or seen in his entire life. And with that fateful move, my career running drugs had begun. It was 1975.

For the next two years I ran millions of dollars of marijuana from Durango to California on countless trips. During this time, I met a few other smugglers through a chain of distributors I had built to help move my product. I began taking trips to other states in Mexico with other smugglers and eventually, I came under the watchful eye of the cartels in the regions where we operated.

In 1979, I was in Culiacan, Sinaloa, Mexico, with a friend I had met in Los Angeles a couple of years earlier. He and I were there at the request of one of our contacts from Guadalajara, Jalisco, Mexico, to be introduced to a man who had an interest in us and our developing skills as smugglers.

We were taken to a ranch about an hour out of Culiacan and parked next to a large rock outcropping. Leaving the truck, my friend Luis and I were walked around the rocks by two men who were soldados, or soldiers. On the other side were two figures on their knees, with cloth bags over their heads. They were bound at the wrists, and in front of them were two shallow graves. Our associate stood behind us with pistols pointed at our backs, and escorted us to stand behind those kneeling, quivering men. He gave us each a pistol and told us to shoot the prisoners in the head without hesitation, or we would "take their place in those graves."

I still vividly remember the crack of the pistol as it went off in my hand. I can still hear the thudding sound of the bullet striking the head of the man before me and see his body twitching in that grave as he fell into it. That was the moment of no return. My life had dramatically changed course, forever. The soldados took our pistols and unloaded the remaining rounds into the dead bodies below us.

When it was over, the one soldado who took my pistol put his hand on my shoulder and said, "Now we trust you." I had just made my bones. I was 26 years old.

From then on, I no longer felt in control of my life. I had become a puppet for the cartel. They used me a few times to run cocaine stateside instead of pot, and by 1982, they had recognized my potential as a tool for developing stateside markets. I still made runs with my other friends, but I knew that men much higher up the ladder had an eye on me.

It was during this time that I met the powerful crime boss, "El Chapo" Guzman.

I was ordered to attend a mafia wedding in Culiacan with my wife at the time, Jeri. When we arrived, we were met at the airport and escorted by two carloads of cartel soldados to a ranch on the outskirts of town. There were several people at the ranch that I had grown to know over the years, former smugglers and family friends.

At this point in my career, I was a boss in the organization. I sat at the main table with the other bosses. Our wives were gathered towards the rear under the protection of armed guards. As the night went on, I noticed that even more armed soldados had appeared, basically surrounding the entire gathering.

A few moments later, El Chapo himself walked in and was greeted with hugs and handshakes. He went to the head table of the wedding couple and their families and presented them with an elaborate gift. I had no idea what was in the box he handed over, but I am pretty sure it was valuable, judging by their shocked expressions.

He then came to the table of bosses, where I was formally introduced to him as "a trusted friend from the Pacific Northwest." He looked me in the eyes and smiled as he shook my hand. There were no words said, but I knew he was memorizing what I looked like. He left shortly after that moment. El Chapo does not stay anywhere for very long.

The next time I met El Chapo was about three months later in a small village called La Junta. I was in Culiacan, discussing my role in moving part of a six-ton shipment of cocaine which was already heading north, when my associate, Jose, received a call. One of El Chapo's people told Jose to go up to the rancho, and to take me. I remember us passing through two cartel checkpoints on our way through the hills above La Junta.

I recall passing through a small town where I heard a woman in grief, crying, screaming, and clutching a small child by her side. As we drove past her, I looked at the doorway of her adobe home, and there, at the base of the door, sat two bloody heads, both male.

There are no words to describe the agony so evident in her screams. But we drove on.

Upon arrival at the site, we were led into a ranch house where El Chapo was waiting. This time, he did talk to me. He was very interested in the Canadian market for cocaine. He asked me about how we were able to get his cocaine across the border, and about the benefit of trading his cocaine for the high-grade marijuana the Canadians grew. He asked me to look into it, then he shook my hand, smiled, and signaled to one of his soldiers to escort me out of the room.

This was the last time I saw El Chapo. This was also the last time I was in the "Lion's Den" (Cartel Land) working for the cartel. Three months later, I walked into the Seattle Attorney General's office to take it all down.

To be perfectly clear, I wasn't some snitch running around telling on people. My targets were specific. My family's safety was paramount in my mind.

However, old habits are hard to break. Because I had lived in Mexico as a young teen, their way of life had imprinted itself on me. I was once told, "The blood of our village pumps in your heart." Others could tell there was something different about me. This was true. I was different. I had become a man of two cultures.

During my drug-running heyday, I knew the three, world-famous Arellano Felix brothers who led the Tijuana Cartel on the border between Mexico and the U.S. south of San Diego. They were competing with the El Chapo cartel on the Sonora border control in what was essentially a cartel war.

Back in 1969, I had met Ramon when his uncle, a drug lord, would come up to visit the man who was responsible for my safety. Ramon and I would ride burros together on the mountain trails, talking like friends. Ramon, who was younger by 10 years, visited with his uncle three times during my time in Durango.

Years later, I was in Acapulco when Pablo Escobar was killed. Ramon's brother, Rafael came in from Colombia and told me his version of what happened to Escobar. He was upset and was on his way to Tijuana to discuss this with his brothers.

Through the early '80s, I had developed a cocaine market extending from the Pacific Northwest all the way across the country to Minnesota. I was moving from a quarter to a third of a ton of cocaine a month. I also established safehouses for stockpiling large loads coming up from the south.

A few years later, I was arrested for the first time. I was convicted of trafficking cocaine and was sentenced to three years in prison. I served my time and was released from Folsom Prison in 1989.

I left California and that prison, fully committed to starting a new life in a town just north of Seattle. I fell into a land deal through a childhood friend of mine and managed to turn a nice profit. With that profit, I purchased other real estate holdings, opened up an antique store in a small community, got married, and started a family. My life was good, and I began to prosper. I had everything I wanted, and I was doing it legally and safely.

However, I always knew the day would come when my old life would come knocking. It eventually did.

Several years into my move, I received a letter with two plane tickets to Las Vegas and $5,000 in cash. I knew better than to refuse, so I took my new wife and went to Vegas. The man I met with was the man I had "made my bones" with years ago, Alfredo. It was now 10 years after I had become trusted by the cartel. Alfredo told me I owed a debt, and to refuse would result in the death of those I loved.

In return for my freedom from their clutches, I agreed to rebuild the empire I had once created for them—along with paying $1,000,000 to clear my "debt." They had sucked me right back into the life I had desperately tried to escape. But my back was against the wall. I had no way out. They knew where I lived. They knew everything about me.

This led to the creation of Operation Northern Exposure in 1991. A joint task force was formed, put together by the federal government specifically to take me down and the network I had helped build. I became the primary target in the Pacific Northwest, and knew my time was limited. Over the next two years, I rebuilt the cartel organization, knowing I was under the watchful eye of the various agencies under the umbrella of the Department of Justice. When the debt was paid, I flew to Culiacan, Sinaloa, Mexico, to inform the soldados my time had come to break away and return to the clean life I so wanted and desired.

Instead, when I arrived back home, two soldados and 350 kilos of cocaine were sitting in a white van in my driveway. They wanted more. My mind was racing at that moment. I had just over $3 million in cash in my bedroom, and I thought seriously about taking off, disappearing from the grid. I knew a plastic surgeon down in Durango, and I had the money to buy a new identity and simply vanish. That was my thought process until my little baby boy walked into the living room with a bottle in his mouth. I did not want this life for him. I didn't want him to spend a lifetime on the run. So, I gave the $3 million dollars to the soldados in the van and sent them and their load back to Los Angeles.

The next morning, I hired the best attorney in Seattle and walked into the Assistant U.S. Attorney's office to officially become a witness. This was the second-biggest turning point in my life. I needed to get away from it, and this was the only way to do that with certainty.

In January 1990, prior to my decision to become an informant, Panamanian dictator Manual Noriega was arrested, and a bank account was seized that I had access to. The account held more than $22 million dollars. It was an established account that I had money in, along with others with whom I had been involved. We thought at that time that our profits were hidden away and secure. But we were wrong. Twenty-two million dollars was gone overnight.

Over the next 19 months, in conjunction with the Drug Enforcement Administration and U.S. Customs, I started naming distributors, mules, and smugglers all the way to the southern regions of Mexico and as far north as Vancouver in British Columbia, Canada.

During the time I was aiding U.S. law enforcement, I was kidnapped in Culiacan by Mexican Federal Agents on the payroll of the cartel. I was in a sting operation, in my car with two guys from that region who had planned to take me to meet a general in the

Mexican Army. He had a helicopter waiting for me at the airport to look at 3,000 kilos of cocaine that he wanted to sell us.

But we never made it to our destination. We were forced off the road. I was pulled out of my vehicle along with the two men, bound, and a black cloth bag was placed over my head. I was dumped into the back of a truck with two other men. I was jabbed with their AK 47s, beaten and kicked and then taken to an undisclosed interrogation site. There, I was isolated from the others and chained to a wall as I heard the screams of the others fade away into a silence. That experience was the most surreal thing that ever happened to me. I was certain I would die in that cell.

A man approached me, put a gun to the side of my head, and pulled the trigger. He cocked the pistol, put it to my head and pulled the trigger again, and again, and again until I started losing focus. Reality no longer felt real.

The next thing I remember was hearing rapid gunfire outside and English-speaking voices yelling, searching. The mask was yanked off my head, and there was a Navy SEAL, holding a picture of me in one hand and looking at me, asking if I was Hal Bradley. I had been badly beaten, and all I could do was nod my head.

I remember the Navy SEAL telling me I was going to be okay, that I was getting out of there. I passed out after that, awakening as I was being loaded into a helicopter and airlifted out. I remember arriving at the U.S. Embassy in Mexico City, being cleaned up, debriefed, the next day being flown into Paine Field in Everett, Washington, and then being home. I learned later that the DEA agent who was working with me had gotten drunk the night before in a brothel in Culiacan and spilled information to a prostitute. All the agents at the Seattle office said was, "It wasn't meant to be."

I was involved in several missions on foreign soil during the 19 months before I entered the federal prison system. I had finally begun making a positive impact. I helped law enforcement capture a drug submarine, and my eventual success was measured in dollars. One DEA agent told me that the cost of cocaine had gone up from $22,000 to $24,000 a kilo in Seattle as a result of diminished supply versus the strong demand.

My story shifts the day of my sentencing. I was standing before a federal judge. As I prepared to hear my sentence, they brought in my counterpart from the Mexican state of Sinaloa. As he walked past me in the courtroom, he turned and said, "You know..." A DEA agent heard his comment and said to me, "Does that mean what I think it means?" I simply nodded. A contract had just been put on me. There were people out to kill me.

I was sentenced to eight years in federal prison, and the next phase of my life began.

The Conversion

Buckley, Washington–October 1994

I was in a holding cell. My wife had just left the jail, telling me she had filed for divorce. "I didn't marry the mafia," she said. And she got up and left.

With the loss of my wife and three children, the weight of eight long years of prison ahead of me, and with a contract on my head, I hit my breaking point. This was my moment of transformation.

In tears, I fell to the floor in my cell, calling out to God to take this burden from me. As I bowed before God, a prisoner came and knelt beside me, and then another prisoner came and knelt on the other side of me, both praying.

At that moment, something inside of me broke. Pain left me. Guilt left me. Fear left me. In the instant of my surrender and true belief, I felt a hunger for knowledge and understanding of God through Christ like nothing I had ever felt before.

Englewood, Colorado, (Correctional Institute Colorado)

I knew I had to begin looking ahead to the new path God gave to me. Upon arrival, I checked into the prison chapel to pick up a Bible for study. (An interesting side note: This Bible has served me well. I used it in my years of seminary studies, the year and a half spent as a nationally certified hospice minister, in my seven years in the pulpit, and for the last 11 years in my ministry in homeless camps, hospital bedside visits, and last rites services. Twenty-four names of the inmates who died under my hospice care are listed in this Bible. The many inmates I prayed for daily are also listed. It includes information on marriages and ordinations I performed as a senior pastor. I still use it today!)

While at Englewood, I abruptly fell very ill. My liver was shutting down, prompting my transfer to the Medical Center for Federal Prisoners in Springfield, Missouri. Upon arrival, I was placed in a medical ward for terminal patients.

I volunteered for what was an experimental drug called Interferon 2B, a medicine designed to eradicate Hepatitis C, which was the diagnosed cause for my liver malfunctioning.

During my months of treatment, my body responded well. While at the ward, I was able to fulfill requirements to become a certified hospice counselor. I aided 24 prisoners through their dying process. Most of my seminary studies through a Pentecostal ministry were completed while sitting in these dying rooms, ministering to these desperately ill inmates.

During this time, I also worked in the prison's education department helping inmates get their GEDs. I also wrote publications for the Hospice Journal Magazine and crammed like crazy to complete my studies.

By my second year, I completed my seminary studies. Johnny Gambino, the famed American mobster, threw my graduation party. By this time, I was also doing interviews for the Springfield newspaper, plus juggling ministry to as many as three dying patients at a time.

In my fifth year, one of the agents who worked with me in various countries during that 19 months before sentencing had me brought back to court and got the judge to reduce my sentence by two years. (He was also the agent who placed me under arrest the day I walked in. Although he retired in 2020, we've stayed in touch and until 2016 worked cases together.)

When I returned from court, I was sent to Leavenworth for my final year of incarceration. During that time, I connected with Hospice of Leavenworth and set up four, 10-week training cycles teaching prisoners the art of caregiving and getting them certified. This work led to interviews with the local newspapers.

The night before I left the prison, I was led into the basement by the friend who had given me the Bible many years before in the Colorado prison. When he flipped on the lights, there were over 100 inmates, staff and outside visitors throwing me a surprise going-away party. This has never been done in the history of Leavenworth.

I had found victory amidst a lifetime of crisis.

I was on my way...

CHAPTER 1:
Expect to Survive

Definition of survival: "*The state or fact of continuing to live or exist, typically in spite of an accident, ordeal, or difficult circumstances.*"

When a potentially catastrophic event occurs, such as a pandemic or economic collapse, – or in my case, being ripped from everything one knows and holds dear – we can find ourselves rebuilding our lives in a manner which warrants immediate action. When such an event presents itself, our approach to that moment can determine whether we enjoy successful recovery – or find ourselves worse off than before. This, in turn, almost always affects all those entwined in our lives. We must focus on our options, and, if possible, any resources we have developed in our lifetime, or we must seek assistance from our community.

However, in a crisis, no resources may be available. You may not have anyone to help you. When that is the case, you must resort to self-dependence, and your ability to summon the strength within yourself. This strength exists inside all of us naturally. It allows us to achieve things that ordinarily would be impossible.

In extreme, life-threatening circumstances, we must respond with an almost-superhuman mindset in order to rise above the norms we are conditioned to and overcome the immediate threat.

This book is about responding to crisis, whatever that may look like. It can come from any angle. It can be a loss of your job. It could be a serious health problem for you or your loved one, or it could be a criminal attack.

Regardless of what kind of crisis you are going through, there is a clear and simple path to avoid disaster – a path to making the crisis work for you. You can find victory in that crisis by using it as an opportunity to make your life better.

I spent the better part of 30 years achieving wins from crises. I have helped countless others overcome their own crises and emerge victorious. My life has included many of these dire situations, and I know they happened to me specifically so that I could pass that knowledge onto other people in my life. And that is what I've done.

I have worked as a grief counselor for nearly 20 years, and I've tried to use my own hardship to show them what I found. No matter how deep the pit of hell you're stuck in might be, the rainbow above you can be attained through your own hard work. The power exists inside you. That is where you find victory.

The Unthinkable Happens

The first step is truly the most difficult: You're faced with a crisis. This can be a life-shattering moment, he kind of nightmare no one expects to befall them.

This type of event is what we fear most in life. People often reject it at first. Something that horrible is nearly impossible to accept immediately.

But no matter how you attempt to push it away, the pain and fallout are unavoidable. The longer you delay, the harder it becomes.

With that in mind, step one is to accept the circumstances as they are. This is the life you are forced to live. Accept it and recognize that this is a situation out of your control. It is a scenario that you have to meet head-on, so that you can take yourself in the necessary direction to climb out of it.

Acceptance is everything because it puts us in a positive direction. We need something to follow in order to reconstruct our life, to make it through whatever chaotic event destabilized it.

The worst thing you can do is refuse to accept the situation. If you fail to accept the situation and try to avoid it, or take an impractical approach, trouble will mushroom. This will only lead to more obstacles that you're going to find yourself confronted with down the road. In many ways, you're digging yourself into a deeper hole.

Meanwhile, as you resist acceptance, your body sends off stress signals. Why? Because you're fighting against something that's inside of you. It's all about internal acceptance. Even if you think you may have accepted this crisis, your body knows the truth. If you are fighting it, or in denial, or trying to pretend like it doesn't matter, your body is going to have a reaction. You're going to be sending off stress signals, and those "fight or flight" signals make the situation worse. In this situation, you're not able to access your higher levels of thinking. These signals impair your decision-making, which is one of the most important tools in your arsenal during a crisis. To fight acceptance is to sabotage your own recovery.

The moment of acceptance is the beginning of recovery. You must understand that there is no going back. This acceptance gives you a direction to start developing the self-discipline to achieve and accomplish whatever is necessary within your own life to overcome and to achieve success. You can begin reconstructing your life.

The External

Just as we as humans can emanate positivity, we also can exude negativity. When we approach a life-crisis scenario with a negative mindset, we emanate that negativity into the world around us. That energy is leaving us. In many ways, it's stolen from our body. This limits your total resources because you are wasting energy that could be applied elsewhere.

Make no mistake, it requires an enormous amount of energy to maintain a negative mindset. It is draining.

More than that, people will pick up on your negativity. That could be extremely detrimental if you're looking for resources to help you surmount the challenge that you find yourself facing. They will feel your energy and reflect it. You have to be willing to move towards the light, and into understanding. This is part of acceptance.

Reflect on your crisis and think to yourself, "I am in this awful situation. I am in this true low point in my life. I need to overcome this crisis through a positive direction that I, alone, can create."

Recognize that only change from within will lead to victory. Every other path is temporary. You need to develop the ability to stay positive, even in worst-case scenarios.

We get confronted in life with some very serious scenarios – some of us more than others. But everyone experiences these moments of extreme stress and anxiety. Even our most capable friends and family members have felt helpless.

If we can convert our negativity into a positive direction from the outset, then new avenues start becoming available. This takes practice, but the result is a much more durable mindset – one that can handle anything.

You may be thinking, "If I accept my situation and try to stay positive, won't that hold me back from escaping?"

To that I say the following: The moment that we embrace a positive direction and mentality, no matter how bad the scenario is, new options are created for us.

Your mindset can dramatically shift your perception of reality in your situation. As long as you accept where you stand and stay resolute in your positivity, you will always find new ways to succeed. This is the phase of not only acceptance, but also of goal setting as you look toward the future instead of back at the past.

You'll find a newfound discipline, one that develops when you begin switching to positive thinking. That discipline starts letting you focus on other objectives, rather than the current situation. Positivity takes this negative scenario and transforms it into something that's actually exciting to look forward to. It's all in your mind. Your perception affects the outcome.

There is also the physical response. Your body feels the weight of that negativity. Negativity festers in our body. It is scientific fact that stress and anger lead to a whole host of physical ailments. The cortisol in your brain literally shortens your lifespan. Stress, and your response to that stress, is as much a threat as the crisis to which you are responding.

The moment you instead accept it, the body takes that weight off. Ask yourself, "How do I get out of this situation? How do I progress – and not only progress, but improve as rapidly as possible in order to return to the fruitful life I once had? How do I come back to that calmness and peace within me?"

Strive to embrace a peace that ensures, even in the face of the greatest of storms, you will come out triumphant on the other end. The beautiful thing is you will emerge a better version of yourself as a result of that experience. These triumphs will transform you in dramatic ways.

When preaching the gospel in the pulpit, I often use the example of Christ on the cross. His suffering, the greatest suffering of all, was so great that he even began to doubt his own Self.

But what happened? He turned to a higher power, The Father, and he said, "Take this bondage from me." At that moment, he had clarity. He had acceptance. He could return to peace. He saved Decimus on the cross beside him. Jesus told him, "This very day you will be with me in paradise."

This happens in our own lives. Our acceptance is felt by the people around us. As a result, their combined energy begins to elevate us out of that pitfall of disparity. We start rising immediately. They say that a rising tide lifts all ships, and the same is true with positivity.

If you put out positive energy, you will start drawing positive energy. Who wants to work with someone who is negative, depressed and continues to focus on negativity? Nobody. Humans, by design, crave cooperation and acceptance. All highly social animals need positivity in order to feel a sense of normalcy.

I have been a grief counselor for 23 years. When somebody comes to me at the moment of their greatest crisis, if I can get them to start looking at the positive aspects and give them objectives to fulfill, they start gaining a different mindset. They can focus on recovery. Their mentality is the biggest driver of their success.

If you are facing a divorce, the loss of a child or parent, or financial collapse from an unforeseen situation, your approach in that moment can be to say, "This will not conquer me. I'm going to take wisdom from this chaotic event. I'm going to use that wisdom to survive. And this wisdom will transcend to others who will help elevate me out of this crisis. I will rise due to the wisdom I gain from this trial."

That reframing is acceptance, and the moment you're able to access something positive, the first step must be acceptance. Your first decision must be to enter into a positive vibration. At that point, you are aligned with the power of nature and the universe and all the people around you, who are also aligned in that positive place.

A Positive Step

With the first step understood, the second step is all about learning to overcome the obstacle from a positive direction – whatever that obstacle may be. Understand that any obstacle can be shared with others in your life. They may have insight or input, and they can assist your progress.

You have control of the environment you're in, as well. If you need to relocate, then do it. A change of atmosphere can drastically improve your outlook and options.

That is the second half of the initial two-step process. The first is acceptance, and the second is finding the positive to overcome the obstacle.

It is crucial that you put yourself in an environment where it's actually hard to go into the negative. The environment that you put yourself in, the people you're surrounded by, they are key to tapping into this positive outlook and holding onto it. They are your anchor in many ways. And that is okay. Part of acceptance is having the strength and humility to lean on others.

But within that, you choose who and what you gravitate towards. You can cling to negativity with others, because misery loves company. However, if you're willing to distance yourself, even if it means isolating yourself from unhealthy relationships, you are able to be objective. You can begin to calm the soul and start progressing in a positive direction with a healthy mindset.

This is where I want to introduce the idea of a higher power. I personally am a Christian, but you can do this with any faith. It can be spiritual, religious, or neither, as long as you feel it can transcend you and your environment.

The objective is to align yourself with an environment that makes you more positive, thus releasing your anxieties. When people are in fearful situations, their minds become clouded, they reimprison themselves in a spiral and the negative environment doesn't allow them to take that moment of pause and calmness within their own soul.

The Higher Power and My Recent Crisis

After this acceptance, an inner direction must be chosen and adhered to. This will help you understand what is happening, and what needs to happen.

I want to highlight this idea by sharing a story. It ties to the life I worked so hard to leave, the one you read in the introduction. Even now, 20 years later, the shadow of my former self haunts me and taints my experience. I share this tale, not for pity, but for you to begin to understand what I mean when I refer to seeing the path ahead.

In the summer of 2020, I had a near-death experience. I was stabbed three times in quick succession by a hitman sent by the cartel I had once shared a table with.

I will go into the story of his attack and my survival in a later chapter. I learned so much from that near-death event. There I was, in a critical moment in my life, and the first thing I thought is that I needed to survive this. How do I survive this critical moment? In my case, I crawled up my stairs, got behind my security gate, locked it, punched in a 911 and was able to allow myself to be saved as I was passing out.

To survive something like that, you must draw on the spirit within yourself and pick yourself up. I'd lost four pints of blood by the time help arrived. I was bleeding out, but I still put together a psychological barrier from the potential end of life as I was facing it.

We all have this inside us. It's almost a supernatural gift that is given to us. Through the universe, we draw from so many different energies, and find that higher power. This spiritual energy is the higher power scenario. It can be used to remove yourself from your environment, or keep you grounded in moments of life and death. It is a driving force of pure will and faith, and that kind of concentration and determination is uniquely powerful. It is capable of amazing things.

In these situations, you should first force yourself to pause. When you take pause, and you calm yourself in the most horrific of moments, other thoughts present themselves to you. Then, there are options. Once you have created options in your chaotic experience, you can reflect on them. You would be amazed how fast they come to light in that moment. Options are your way out.

When I was stabbed, I thought I was dead. But 45 minutes later, I came out of the fog like Lazarus. I mean, I rose from the dead, literally. Covered in blood and barely conscious, I awoke. The first thing I did was find an area of safety. The second thing I did was secure that safe zone. And then the third thing I did, which was within seconds, was reach out to a resource that could come to my aid in that moment.

Of course, this is much harder in practice. When you are in shock and trauma and smack-dab in the middle of an unfolding crisis, the mind desperately searches and seeks out something to cling to. This is where another factor, practice and mental preparation, both become so very helpful. Running through these types of events ahead of time can mean the difference of a few seconds. In a crisis, those seconds may be what changes a failure into a victory.

After you have accepted the circumstances that you find yourself in, you must condition yourself to recognize resources that can be made available as a result of this new environmental change. Once you've accepted something, you have identified it. Once you have identified the crisis, it's time to take a step back and take a breath. Use your improved mental space to make an accurate read on the situation.

Take that breath, take that moment, and think, "Okay, what are my options?" You have to drag yourself out of a shock scenario. You must act quickly, as soon as you find yourself in these scenarios. You must depend on the basic survival instinct.

What does it mean to pause and take stock of things? It is defined by subtle moves, like taking that first breath to still the mind. Such a practice is so useful, I want to give you an exercise to practice this still-breathing technique.

It is only through practice that any of this will become effective in the event of a true crisis. First, tune into your breath. And by tune in, I mean turn your attention inward and focus on your breath. Allow all the other thoughts to just fade away. Watch how the breath comes in as you inhale and watch how your lungs expand, and your chest lifts. Feel the sensation of the air rushing past your lips and nostrils. And then, when you exhale, watch how your chest now sits down and your lungs go back to the smaller size. And watch your breath like this for three full, slow cycles. Stay as focused on your breathing and body as you can.

Breathing creates. When you oxygenate, the body responds to the oxygenation and calms down. You're regenerating yourself and diminishing whatever panic you might have felt. The breath is creating oxygen for the body, and you're bringing oxygen to the brain.

Most importantly, the breathing exercise takes you out of the fight or flight response. Typically, if you look at somebody who's in fight or flight mode, they're panicking. Their breath is shallow. They are flustered. Their mind isn't as sharp as it is ordinarily. Part of that is the poor breathing technique. The breaths are shallow and quick. By slowing your breath down, you tell your nervous system that, "I am not in danger, I am okay." It shifts you out of fear into calm.

Your focus should be natural breathing exercises. Calm breathing generates calm thinking. Calm thinking leads to better decision-making.

That is the exercise. That is the first main idea of this book. This is something that will be re-emphasized throughout the book. Expect to keep coming back to this idea. You are starting with this because everything else in the rest of the book goes back to this idea.

If you go into fight or flight, if you start to breathe shallow, catch yourself and go back to this breathing exercise. The breath is the oxygen, the fuel. It will be the fuel that propels your mind in healthy directions.

Breathing techniques enhance calmness and clarity. The brain gets oxygenated and the body becomes comfortable and compatible. A realignment of mindset is the outcome.

In any situation of panic, you have to find one thing to focus on. Begin the breathing technique, and this will relax you. Options can then develop and be considered.

The Will to Go On

The next idea may seem obvious at first, but it is absolutely essential. You must expect to survive. You must want it and want it badly.

How many people do you think find themselves in a crisis and simply collapse? They think, "This is it. I'm done. This is the end for me." They crumble in the face of pressure. What are the odds of them getting out of that situation if they just accept their fate as sealed?

Acceptance isn't always a pleasant thing. The situation you face may make you question everything: your spirituality, your capability, even yourself. But if you can maintain the will to push through and get to a place of moving towards a positive mindset, anything can happen.

Remember, it is a beautiful universe. It is an absolutely incredible place to be existing, especially right now, when you are confronted and faced with so many things that are not so beautiful. You can turn them into statements of beauty!

You, and all humans, are made up of three components. You are body, you are mind, and you are soul or consciousness. Those are the three components that are out of alignment in moments of crisis. Learning to realign as quickly as possible is the best way to ensure you're working in harmony with your true self.

The stories that you hear in fables and ancient texts always involve a crisis. As the story unfolds, you learn how the hero or heroine overcomes the crisis. This inspires humanity.

You have an opportunity to create that inspirational story in your own life. A crisis provides your moment, your opportunity to achieve and become what you read about and the stories you tell others. This is victory!

CHAPTER 2: Finding Resources to Survive in a New Environment

While the central theme so far has been identifying and locating potential resources, this chapter is about exploration. We are going deeper. I want to walk you through, step by step, how to find and take advantage of resources – what to look for, and how your perception can drastically alter your outcome.

Once you have accepted your catastrophic scenario and calmed the soul through your breathing exercises, you can focus on your primary objectives. You must find a shelter or an environment that is relaxing – whatever can help you stabilize your surroundings.

This chapter is about finding resources to survive your new environment. No matter how difficult it gets, you cannot give up. You cannot accept the notion that this is going to take you out. Your will to survive and your desire to turn this crisis into a victory will give you the strength to overcome everything.

What's the first thing you do? You create an image of yourself that people will see worthy of helping. You want to position yourself in a fashion that

Finding Resources to Survive in a New Environment

will prompt people to think, "Something about this person makes me want to reach out. I can feel their energy, and I want to hear their story and possibly be there to assist them." You want to appear to be someone worth helping who also helps themselves. How you present yourself in that moment will determine the options that will be available to you.

The second step, after securing this space and assistance, is to gain knowledge as rapidly as possible about the location of assets necessary for survival. You have to know what you need, so make a mental list of what you need to achieve your immediate goals. You resource these opportunities through people.

Sometimes the situation is bigger than a personal crisis. As I write this, the pandemic in 2020 has deeply damaged the world economy. Poverty levels are at 8 million and rising. Food and housing insecurity are a very real fear for millions of Americans.

Any economic crisis or steep recession could catapult millions of people into a similar, dire situation. If this happens on a mass scale, it certainly limits your personal options.

For instance, there may be no room at any shelter. All the food banks, American Red Cross and Salvation Army may not have any resources left. They may have already given out all the clothing, they may have given out all the medical aid packets. This is where self-reliance becomes crucial.

I'm taking this to an extreme, so that everyone may take guidance from this book to understand that the most valuable asset that you have in your recovery of life is your own self. How you approach the situation that you find yourself in, in the moment, is of great significance. You are your best resource.

Where do you find those resources? That depends. Who do you know? Do you have a family member or a lifelong friend? Do you have somebody who has the knowledge to acquire resources? You must have the basics. You have to eat and sleep and survive. You must seek an environment where you don't have to fear for your life.

As a career counselor, I've seen these situations many times. Even in homeless shelters, I have seen the fears and concerns around keeping possessions safe.

You must extract yourself from those types of environments. Even if it means isolation. These are survival tools you must keep in mind if you find yourself facing crisis.

These tragic situations can happen overnight. They can happen instantly. Over the years I've met with many people who had great jobs and all of the sudden they've lost the job, and they've lost their

Finding Resources to Survive in a New Environment

resources. Last month they had an apartment and a job, this month they might be sleeping under a picnic table at some park along with 10,000 other people. All of a sudden, access to what they need to exist becomes extremely limited.

Many people judge those who experience a drastic lifestyle downshift. A tendency to blame the individual may surface, as though they did something to put themselves in that challenging environment.

Judgment of this type is human nature, and human nature is driven by ego. The false ego can often misguide people, creating negative thoughts about others, or a negative spiral downward. We must overcome and stay humble. We must realign our thoughts with an acceptance of the universe in a peaceful and loving, compassionate manner.

The first 30 years of my life I grew up around the cartels and death and destruction and hatred. Everything was driven by money and violence. I lived and worked under very cruel and dangerous people.

Then one day, a chaotic event occurred in my life when I found myself on my knees in a jail cell heading to prison, crying out saying, "I can no longer take this." At that point, I accepted my situation, and then I found an energy source to direct it to. That energy source became my resource. Another resource is your approach. Having the ability to turn to guidance is a resource.

Optional resources must be acceptable within our own current life scenario. You have to have faith in yourself, as you are seeking the resources that you need to exist.

But most importantly, you have to be OK within your own self. You must be tough. You must survive rejection, you must be able to survive self-blame during a guilt syndrome with thoughts such as, "My God, I'm here because I could have done this in a different way a year or two ago." We're describing here another important resource that is not a physical resource. Aligning yourself to an environment where you can maintain your self-image is a crucial. This is all-important.

Then you need a place. Once you get a place, you need the basics to keep the body going, which, of course, include food and water.

Putting off the right energy, as mentioned earlier, is important at this point. You want to create scenarios that draw people to you. Your aim is to attract anyone who might help you with resources necessary to continue onto the next stage.

Everything that you've done in the first chapter is designed to make this easier. By keeping your breath calm, you will stay out of the "fight or flight" mentality. You will appear as approachable and calm to other people. You will emanate a positive outlook, which is attractive to other positive people.

Creating a Feeling

I want to illustrate this idea with the story of my attack. Even a person of pure hatred, sent with the sole purpose of ending my life, can use this outward energy to lull people into a false sense of security.

I was at my home when he came upstairs. I was between him and the security gate when he explained that he was a tow truck driver, and that he had backed into this yellow Corvette Stingray parked outside. My car. He said that one of my tenants had told him that it was mine. It was an easy story for me to fall into, but the first thing I noticed was his hygiene. It sticks in my mind. He smelled right. His clothing looked right. He had a baseball cap pulled down at an angle that made it impossible to see his face. That should have been my first reg flag. That should have sent the alarm bells ringing in my head.

Ten years ago, I would have never put myself in that situation. But he relaxed me. His energy lulled me off guard. And if a hitman can achieve so much with energy, think of how you'll be able to improve your situation with similar skill. The power of displaying positive outward energy is not to be underestimated.

He created a desire in me to open up that security gate. I agreed to follow him down the stairs to assess the damage to my Corvette. He created that. His energy evoked that feeling within me.

Note that I am a man with a PhD and 20 years of experience surviving in a drug smuggling environment. I had a lifetime of experience, and he fooled even me. He was calm in his approach. He was presentable in his approach. This information was reliable and made sense to me. Because I'd awakened out of a dead sleep to answer the door, I walked right down the stairs and almost right into my death.

The next time I am attacked, it will probably be a drive-by in a Safeway parking lot. Something faster. But I'm not worried about those fears. They don't influence or affect my life. I'm just more aware and more compassionate, trying to pay attention to all things around me.

You must remember, I'm a former smuggler, and my ability to create this outward energy was a big part of my success. I was never once busted smuggling. I made several hundred international crossings during my career. It is because I was totally aware of my environment and my influence on that environment. That awareness helped me survive. And my awareness saved my life in that attack – awareness and dumb luck! But I will not live in fear. I will only feel compassionate and grateful for being alive.

CHAPTER THREE:
Retrain Your Thinking

The first two chapters focused on preparing for survival post-crisis and securing the necessary resources to ensure success. You have already begun to reshape the way you approach the crisis and your response to that pressure.

Now we'll build on that transformation. You must begin to prepare your consciousness and mindset to transform your life accordingly. This is another difficult step, but I want to help you begin that process. This section focuses on coping, and coping mechanisms.

For millions of Americans, the pandemic has been a true crisis. People lost jobs, their homes, and their loved ones. Others were forced into a kind of isolation for months on end. It was extremely overwhelming. This massive sociological shift left many with deep feelings of hopelessness. Depression in our country rose to an all-time high.

I conducted a counseling session here with a woman who is dealing with pandemic-related anxiety and feelings of hopelessness. This woman had become overwhelmed and felt nothing but dread and despair since the pandemic started. As of this writing, we are in month eight of the COVID season and she, like so many others, felt overwhelmed with emotion.

People continue to seek counseling with me who are financially crippled. People are coming to me because they've lost contact and communication with other people within their circle of life. They don't know what to do.

The solution I offer is to divert this overwhelming experience. We must find a way to reduce the sheer size of the crisis in our minds. We can then take that seemingly insurmountable situation and turn it into something slightly more manageable. This allows us to cope with that pressure.

Everything feels overwhelming in a pandemic, or any crisis. Emotions are heightened. People go into panic mode, and that panic spreads, further spiraling the situation.

The first step is to take that turmoil and shrink it. Success and the ability to overcome happens in small doses. Learn to take it on a little bit at a time. Then, before you know it, you've plowed straight through. It all starts with tiny steps, and that is okay. Part of adopting the correct mentality is understanding that the process is an incremental one.

Anytime you recover in your life, it is always because you didn't take it all on in the moment. Catch your breath for a spell. Do the breathing exercise from chapter one. Then, reduce the size of whatever is conflicted within you. Look at only the very next steppingstone in front of you.

Using the pandemic as a real-world example, you need to break down all of the factors standing in your way. No matter how long the list, seeing it all in one place always makes it feel more manageable. It frames the issues into something less daunting.

When considering a pandemic, for example, there are a few immediate issues that need addressing. First off, are you infected? If you are infected, what steps are you taking to recover? Both mentally and physically. Take all the factors and reduce them to actionable steps.

You can't mentally take on the pandemic as a whole. You have to take on an initial goal to start reducing the overwhelming effects, one piece at a time.

In a pandemic, the first thing to ensure survival is to separate ourselves from potential exposure. Next, we have to work to shrink it even further. We can start helping others self-isolate. It does no good to shrink down something like this and try to avoid exposure if everyone else in your life is being exposed regularly. They have to take the same advice.

The problem with that is that humans are powerfully connected to one another. One of the significant under-the-radar problems people are dealing with now is that they are separated from their loved ones. They are lonely, and that affects their mental state. It's human nature to bond, to connect, to be connected. It is a natural reaction to be in touch with other people and to be connected to other people.

How do you reduce that longing? You can reduce that by retraining your thoughts. However, it doesn't happen overnight. You have to do that in progressive stages.

Of course, you want to stay connected to your friends, your family, but you also need to put a mental barrier around yourself. When someone else heads towards anxiety and panic, you need a level of protection because panic spreads. If one person goes into panic, often more people follow, especially when tensions are already heightened.

As mentioned in an earlier section, if you go into panic, you lose touch with the higher levels of consciousness. You need these in order to solve the problem and think clearly.

You have to build a place to take all of this anxiety, where you can constructively start diminishing the anxiety. Your higher power is a place: your faith, your conscious belief, something greater than you that you can go to as a comfort zone to survive such moments of crisis that come into all of our lives.

Once you reduce, you must next identify the strongest components to serve as your focus. Imagine for a moment the worst possible outcome during a pandemic. For example, let's say you experience a financial collapse, and find yourself stranded from your family. You're completely cut off.

Now there are two major roadblocks in this already-terrible situation. You must immediately latch onto one of the three roadblocks and start working constructively to a peaceful, efficient solution. Only then can you start working on the next component of the three you've identified in this crisis scenario. You have to break it down. You have to take it one piece at a time.

Let me put it another way. Muhammad did not move the mountain in one day. He took pieces of it to move the mountain. But in the end, he was victorious. You have to encompass that spirit.

There are statements and there are components to every crisis. The way to successfully become victorious at the end of this scenario is to identify each independent roadblock, have the ability to take that and find a way to make peace with it, and move on. Over and over. You're allowing the crisis to be seen and felt. You process it, and now it's no longer as overwhelming and unbearable. It's something that you can manage and accept. This is part of the retraining. You are re-establishing a pattern of success that can transform your mindset when applied correctly.

A big part of this work is training your mind ahead of time to handle any crisis, and to become victorious through crisis. Then, when you find yourselves in a crisis, you will respond quickly and accurately. You will break the crisis into manageable pieces, and work for solutions and acceptance.

You will also find peace and acceptance much faster this way. It will come almost immediately, because you have created a victorious first step, and your goal is to come through this catastrophic event. That goal and that willingness goes a long way toward acceptance.

The Power of Knowing

Make no mistake, your crisis is not going away overnight. The pandemic has been a period of all-time crisis. At this time, people everywhere are desperately seeking resources to help them get through this tumultuous time of great change and upheaval.

A major resource in this age is information. Information is something you need to rigorously seek and vet, because information gives you answers to important questions.

On the flipside, false information is one of the more dangerous ways to be exploited during a crisis. People working against your interests are a major obstacle, and identifying their motives is crucial to success. You need as much context and information as you can get during periods of turmoil, and misleading or false information from any source may only widen your void.

A crisis breeds a level of desperation, and people often try to take advantage of desperate people. The more you know, the less can be used against you. Knowledge truly is power.

By picking up this book, you have already shown that you are open to receiving the right information. But in this day and age, all sources should be given more scrutiny than ever.

As the Bible says, "Even the very elect can be deceived." Humans have a natural willingness to accept the information presented – especially when it reaffirms what they are hoping is true. You have to make sure that the information has been validated, regardless of source, to ensure that you are, in fact, being guided in the right direction. This is part of retraining your mind. You must constantly be checking and rechecking your sources, assumptions, and resources.

Preparation and anticipation are two of your greatest assets. They prevent you from setting yourself up for failure. Instead, you set yourself up for success, and that, in itself, is major progress.

Expect Victory

If the first step is "Expect to Survive" and all that comes with that idea, the next step is to "Expect to be Victorious." This takes your shifting mindset and pushes it a step further.

You should be actively working towards a victorious solution. This requires only your own, independent ability to segment the crisis and accomplish the numerous goals that you set. Expect to be victorious through each of these segments!

As you get to the end of your obstacles, a new challenge begins. You've broken it down. You've gone through each one. You've integrated a new mindset.

From there, you must take this new acceptance and move into the next phase of our recovery and what you see as your own successful outcome. You have taken your mind out of anxiety and broken down these chunks into pieces that you can accept, integrate, and find peace with.

Most importantly, you have done the work and identified each segment, each component of this overwhelming event. You have identified each part of it. Now you have solved, segment-by-segment, the problem at hand, and found a solution that fits our victory.

Every time you do this, you raise our self-esteem. Every win is a boost in confidence and peace. You are proving that you are not just able to handle a crisis but come through it victoriously. This is something you are proving to yourself as much as anyone else.

This is a large part of retraining your mindset for success: being willing to applaud your own accomplishments and giving yourself the self-love and support you deserve.

Your confidence and the acceptance of your ability to see yourself through this becomes naturalized within. As your confidence grows, so does your success. The two are tied together, and that is why a stronger mindset leads to a brighter future.

Expecting a victorious outcome is the first step towards seeing that vision realized.

CHAPTER FOUR:
Implementation

Every person who ever became strong – strong in character, spiritual strength, and self-esteem – has gone through this process of overcoming a crisis. More than that, they have become strong because they found victory in crisis.

Any natural weaknesses must be overcome and eliminated. In many ways this process is similar to converting coal into diamond. Coal transforms only under immense pressure, and in the process emerges more durable and beautiful than ever. This is also how humans become strong and resilient. Through this process, you are on the path of becoming a diamond. You will be unbreakable.

That is the central theme of this book. You can take a catastrophic event and turn it into a wonderful, beautiful, successful moment in your life. One that only enhances your understanding of yourself and your place in the world.

This chapter moves into the middle of the metamorphosis, as you begin to implement the resources that have been made available.

Implementation

Once you have accepted your transformation, you have acquired new resources. The journey up until this point has been about mental acceptance, finding peace, and becoming that diamond through these pressures that have shown up in your life. And now you will find that there are new resources available.

This accumulation of resources has developed as a result of not only our acceptance, but our success in aligning with that which has been placed before us during such an event.

What do you do with these resources? You should start enabling your immediate environment – and understand that this environment is not just physical, but also metaphysical.

You are body, mind, and soul in equal parts. These are the three components of who you are, and each component is a resource. You have to balance them. These are the truths that you find yourself living in. The physical body can thrive as the other two suffer, and vice versa. You must remain aligned and balanced in order to truly find post-crisis success.

To be resourceful after acceptance, you have to take this new approach. You must utilize what you have learned. That is your primary resource. This process has taught you something – even if you don't know it yet. You have now learned an approach, not only to accept the catastrophic event that you find yourself in, but how to maneuver and manipulate your daily life through that in a positive direction.

There's no greater resource out there than your acceptance. That is the greatest resource. The other resource, of course, is finding agencies or groups that might be able to lift you up or benefit you in your advancement through this. But bear in mind, if you are amid a catastrophic event, you may not have the Red Cross. You may not have the Salvation Army. You may not have the neighbor next door.

You may not have family members who can take on some of the burden through the process. You may not have the standard resources you've been comfortable with and accustomed to your entire life. All of that could've been washed away in the blink of an eye. So, what do you do?

The greatest resource is your self-development. Self-development will see you through to a victorious conclusion.

Moving Past

After confronting the first major obstacle in the crisis, accepting it, and downsizing it, you can now control your response moving through and past it. This resource is the manifestation of acceptance.

You can't afford to get ahead of yourself or feel despair by how much is left. The ideal response is to be calm in the eye of the storm. Aim for being perfectly balanced, and one with your positive mindset.

The acceptance, the understanding, and the removal of conflict within yourself is a major resource. You have removed the conflicted moments. You did that by taking it on in small pieces. You accomplished success in each scenario, and as a result, the greatest resource now is how you maneuver and manipulate your direction from that moment. Whatever it is that you're going through, you have to survive it.

Part of that survival isn't physiological. A great deal of that survival is your psychological approach to the day-to-day encounters that you have ahead of you, because now your world has forever changed. It changed in the blink of an eye.

We are being tested like no other civilization, and we stand at a truly unique point in history. So many people feel overwhelmed because not only do they lack answers, they have not learned a path to achieve peace within themselves.

Dealing with crisis is brand new to many people. They don't know that the process will be transformative. It will alter them for the better. It rarely feels that way in the moment, but that is part of the reason I wrote this book. I want to help you see down the road a bit further.

The first step begins with calming the soul. Once we calm the soul, we can confront anything!

Networking

There are over seven billion people on this planet right now. All of them have doubts, fears, and very real concerns. Connecting with as many of these people as possible is an effective way to build towards victory.

Now every problem has various segments, as you've already identified. For instance, in the pandemic, parents are stuck at home taking care of their children and can't go to work.

There are two different segments in that statement. Children are at home, and parents can't go to work. A network can be a solution to one or more of your problems.

How do you send your children to school without contracting a virus and bringing it back home? How do you go back to work? You have to find resources and answers to all kinds of tricky questions. It always helps to have a larger network.

Your spouse may be one of your primary resources. The Bible tells us "two become one" in the eyes of God in marriage. Whenever I marry couples, I sit down with them and say, "The two of you were designed in body, mind, and soul to join together as one. The physical part of man and woman is to join. The mental part of the man and a woman is to complement and create together. Then the spiritual part is to give glorification to God or your creator or however you want to title him."

You survive as a result of having them connected to your life. It's amazing the knowledge and the wisdom that you gain as a result of this communing. The community strengthens us and embolden us – and can make us wealthier in the end.

From a biological standpoint, humans are extremely social creatures. We live and we survive in tribes. Humans alone in the wild did not survive for very long. We are not equipped to survive as lone animals. Biologically, we need other humans. At our most fundamental level, we crave acceptance and connection.

In the Bible, Adam was never without Eve. We are designed to be side by side. We are designed to be a collective. We are designed to never separate ourselves from the flock. The flock survives by protecting each other.

We as humans do the same thing. As a group, we are more comfortable facing a crisis. We need a group in order to survive and thrive. But we need to understand conscious networking. We must surround ourselves with others who are positive and optimistic and who can help turn these crises into victory. We must choose to be with others who are on a similar path.

My networking experiences literally saved my life on several occasions. You may find yourself in a similar position someday. Perhaps you already have. I was able to connect and network in any situation I found myself in – even prison. Those skills are the reason I am alive today.

With a lot of moving parts, it can be difficult to begin building connections. Perhaps you know no one in your environment. My process always began with vetting a person. That is obviously much harder to do in prison, but there are ways. Everyone will show you who they are if you let them.

In the 1980s when I was arrested and taken to Folsom Prison, I had never been to jail. There I was, catapulted into an environment where people were being stabbed four or five times a day. Death and serious injuries were daily occurrences in that prison back then. It was one of the darkest times in my life.

When I first arrived on the bus, I was taken into the sally port at Folsom Prison. By the time I got there, I had already discerned two or three people on the bus that had personalities similar to mine. They were going there for similar reasons, and I felt a kind of immediate kinship. I started seeking out people who were not conflictive to my purpose. My goal was simply surviving my jail time.

That experience was pure horror. Every decision I made and every move I made revolved around survival. I was completely inexperienced with the prison system. I wasn't a person who grew up in jails and juvenile centers. I never grew up around violence. I grew up around a decent family, and suddenly found myself catapulted into an environment where, if you blink at the wrong guy, you're dead.

We had gangs from Southern California – the Bloods, the Crips, the Surs, the Norteños, the Border Brothers – alongside a melting pot of career criminals. When I would go to the shower, I would go with a group of four or five guys. When I'd go to the chow hall, I would move with a group of four or five guys.

At no point ever in that environment would allow myself to be independent. I would verify a threat indirectly by talking to people that were connected to that threat. I would find out as much as I could from other inmates, guards – anyone. The staff was a major resource. The staff had been there forever and a day, and knew every single inmate. I made sure to vet everyone I interacted with thoroughly. This was, after all, the mid-80s. It was a time when they were rounding up and incarcerating multiple gang members from various gangs. Today, they have other methods to diminish the violence and hostile incidents in the prison system.

My biggest resource in that environment was my own approach to that situation. I accepted that I was there because of my own mistakes. I resolved to control as many factors as I could, when I could – and accept the rest.

When I first arrived, I was briefed with the rest of the new inmates. They took us down to orientation and said very simply, "You're not in the downtown county jail anymore. You're now in Folsom Prison. This is it. This is the end of the road." Every single person there was a potentially dangerous threat to my existence, until I started maneuvering.

You've got to maneuver through your environment, and you got to discern collectively and intellectually every momentary benefit.

My next biggest asset was a willingness to listen. In a crisis situation, rely on people with more experience than you. Lean on their expertise until you get your feet under you.

That's what I did. I would connect with people who had done time in prison before, people who appeared to be on good terms with the entire community. They seemed to not be noticed. They could move through the environment seemingly undetected – and I wanted that.

Implementation

I would latch onto people who knew the ropes, I survived because of it. My smuggling background made me a valuable asset to many factions within the prison. Before long, I was untouchable. Everyone knew not to mess with me. I was useful, and thus indispensable.

I used my former resources that I had self-taught and made myself a benefit to organizations in the prison world. These people were ruthless, but by becoming a tool to be wielded, I survived. That is the only reason I am alive today.

In a sense, this is the next step of resource accumulation. You become a resource, which makes you both valuable and gives you leverage. That is how I got out of Folsom Prison.

When you become a resource to others, you're transcending this idea of crisis. You're tapping into a power bigger than you, and now you are of service. You become an asset. Once you become an asset, you become of value. Everything in prison and in life is about value.

In a crisis, becoming an asset removes obstacles that you were formerly contending with. Once you become an asset instead of a liability, once you have something to offer to the mix, others are willing to cooperate. You build your network faster this way, as well.

When I suddenly found myself embroiled in the drug trade in central Mexico at 16, I worked as fast as I could to become an asset. I started learning as much as I could about the business of growing and smuggling marijuana into the United States. I built an advantage for myself through relentlessness until I had real bargaining power. I became something of worth, something to protect, something to develop, and something to rely on.

This may sound like it doesn't apply to you, but these ideas are universal. Every crisis breeds opportunity. Every crisis opens up doors that you may not have known existed prior to the event. What you need to do is find small, serial opportunities surrounding your crisis and capitalize on them to your advantage that will make you beneficial to others.

This goes back to networking and information. You learn the event, you study the event, and then you capitalize on the knowledge that you pulled out of that situation by turning it into a useful component that adds value to others who are with you.

If everybody contributes in small way to the group, what happens to the group? They become stronger together. They become more valuable together. As a team, they gain in both power and influence.

Implementation

A crisis can hit at any moment. People who were living perfect, normal lives may all of a sudden be flung into chaos.

That's what homeless camps started out as. A week prior, they may have been living in a comfortable house with a normal lifestyle. Then all of that vanished and simply surviving is their aim.

This book is another example of that service and opportunity in a crisis.

By becoming an asset, you can rebound from any crisis. By networking, you can identify places where you can shape your value and seize those opportunities. Alignment is essential with other resources that you have created in this moment of your life. The alignment is essential, based on the creation of these other components that you have brought that you are comfortable with, can identify with, and can use to grow.

CHAPTER FIVE:
Acquiring Basic Needs

We turn our attention to the absolute essentials. These are the pieces that allow you to continue living and breathing. When thinking of Maslow's hierarchy of needs, these are the components that make up the foundation of the pyramid.

Food, shelter, and hygiene – you need to make sure that you have all of these needs taken care of. These needs fulfill a purpose beyond immediate survival, but that is the major driving factor.

Obviously, food and shelter are critical as you put yourself back together and prepare for this new change. But don't you always feel better when you're clean? You are more prepared to go into the next step when you are in the right mental space as you begin this process of rebuilding your life.

Arguably, the most important reason to maintain hygiene is the psychological boost it offers. A spiritual and mental lift comes when you raise your self-esteem. This self-esteem is critically important whenever you are confronted with a catastrophic event.

I want to reiterate this importance of growing and maintaining your self-esteem. No matter how far you get knocked down, self-esteem seems to be a principal enemy in getting back up. I use self-esteem, not in the sense of being prideful, but to mean never losing faith in yourself and your ability to escape a situation.

I always try to instill in those I'm helping through a crisis that staying clean will make them feel so much better and ready to tackle any obstacle. The mental switch is enormous, and it makes a world of difference.

Self-esteem is partly responsible for how hard you work to escape a crisis. The better you feel about yourself and the higher your self-worth, the more confident and motivated you'll be to change your environment for the better.

What makes this so challenging is that you likely won't be in your normal mindset. This won't be business as usual. You'll be in an environment and a situation that you've never been in before, and you'll likely find yourself extremely sidelined or sidetracked as a result. The standard behavioral healings and recoveries you ordinarily use may not be available. You need anything you can hold onto in order to maintain a sense of normalcy.

When you cleanse the body, you also begin cleansing the mind. Everyone knows how refreshing a long shower can be after a hard day. The same principle applies in a crisis event, but it is even more pronounced. Becoming clean will boost your self-image and allow you to feel a small return to normalcy. It is cathartic. And it brings you back toward a centered headspace.

Ultimately, this is why hygiene is so critical. It helps improve your mental state, and that, above all else, is the key to survival in a crisis.

Surviving an extravagant circumstance comes from the calming of the mind. However, the mind doesn't calm if the body isn't prepared to calm it. First you must address the immediate biological needs. This includes rest. This includes putting yourself in an environment where you feel secure and safe. With those out of the way, the mind can focus on the other, equally pressing tasks at hand.

In a practical sense, it is also important to be cleansing the body in order to stop the spread of any viruses. We live in a modern world that has been dominated by a pandemic for nearly a year. This new virus will get into your body and actually take over.

But you have ways to keep the virus out – washing your hands and using a mask. By washing with soap and water, you are breaking down the virus so that it can't enter into your body. Washing regularly stops the spread of the virus. So, if you aren't washing regularly, not only does it impact your self-esteem, but it's also keeping you open to having these pathogens, these viruses, enter into your body.

You need to protect your body as a sacred vessel. It needs to stay clean and pure and free of the viruses.

With that in mind, it is equally important to remove yourself from other people who are not hygienic. The pandemic is spreading due to person-to-person contact. You need to remove yourself from an environment if you see that somebody is sick or ill, because if they sneeze, if they cough or even if they speak, there is a chance of exposure. Masks are a major benefit, but even they are not 100 percent effective. Use proper distancing guidelines and limit your interactions with any potential victims as much as possible.

You must try and eliminate any possibility of exposure. This is not only done in the cleansing, but in the separation and distancing processes that are being recommended by the CDC and other medical sources. Follow guidelines and separate from other people who may be compromised.

In cleansing the body, you are also cleansing your spirituality, and opening up a door to a calm mind. Only there can you start the recovery process. Hygiene is a principled, primary, and effective first step, to catch one's breath, regroup and take on and confront whatever scenario presents itself.

You engage your mind after having cleansed your flesh and cleansed your body, and in doing so you are also cleansing the mind to accept the circumstances.

You must also steel your mind for isolation, which can make you feel disconnected and lonely. Do the best you can under the circumstances. Take the memories and build upon them a relationship that is temporary, but still fulfilling. This allows you to stay connected to those you cherish.

Having been a prisoner, having been through countries where I've been in hiding for weeks at a time, I understand the disconnection that people can be confronted with.

Another vital resource is water. Water is an essential, life-sustaining requirement. You can go without food, depending on body weight for as many as 40 days, but your body cannot stay alive after four days without water. You need to acquire water, maintain the supply, and drink it regularly. Ensure it's treated if you're in an environment where you don't know the source.

If you live in a big city, the water is filtered before it comes into your home. If you're out of the country, or in an environment unfamiliar to you, you need to know exactly where your water is coming from. If needed, you'll have to boil the water to prevent yourself from getting sick. Drinking water is far more important than consuming food, especially given the circumstances that you may find yourself in.

Staying hydrated is vital to staying healthy. You should know exactly how much water you should consume every day, based on body weight and height. Water controls the rhythm of our blood. Water also controls our ability to think and respond quickly and accurately. If the body has a shortage, the body responds to that. And what happens when your body responds? The mind follows.

When you're getting your water and your shelter and your food, you have to be mindful of that which you are in creation. You are a body, you are a mind, and you are a soul. You must strive to keep those three together in equality and in unity. So, when you're feeding one, in essence, you are focusing on the feeding and rebuilding the other two.

Correct Consumption

When in a state of stress, the temptation can be high to turn to artificial relief. It is understandable that one would desire a break from the tension and constant pressure. This can be in the form of hard drugs, but alcohol, cigarettes, sugary foods all can offer pleasure in the moment – but at a cost. They can present real dangers to vulnerable people, and they can and have destroyed countless lives.

People turn to these sources of relief when they feel they are unable to cope. They feel they can't face the reality of their situation. That is part of human nature. People tend to run and hide from stress. When it is significant, they desire something soothing and familiar, even if they know with 100 percent certainty that it is harming them.

You have to replace these temptations with something else. That replacing is done through the self-motivated discipline of being able to modify that which is within your reach.

If you know you are susceptible to a vice, you must put yourself in a position where it is IMPOSSIBLE to access that vice. But more important, you must put something in its place, without leaving a void. Otherwise you'll crave that vice, and it will dominate your thoughts.

A new, healthier outlet can drastically change your path. Remodify your thinking and turn something ordinary into something that you actually look forward to enjoying.

Addiction

As a counselor, I've helped countless people understand and eventually overcome their addiction. I've seen lives destroyed and rebuilt, families mended, and victims from every imaginable walk of life.

If you are dealing with an addiction or know someone going through such a tragedy, my advice for you is this. First and foremost, accept the fact that you are going to have to completely disconnect with this mechanism that has been controlling you physiologically. This familiar, intimate connection must be severed, because it is literally overwhelming all other faculties in its infliction.

You have to prepare yourself mentally for this disconnect. Losing this outlet, this escape that has aided you throughout the crisis, is an inherently uncomfortable event. Even excluding the physical side effects that come with addiction, the mental toll it takes is potent and can be devastating.

In ordinary circumstances, this addiction can be potentially mitigated. The fallout can be shielded by your environment and enablers.

But this all changes during a crisis. When things go wrong, this addiction becomes the worst kind of void. It saps your resources, including energy and mental strength, and offers nothing in return except short-term relief.

The question becomes: how do you fight the impulses and the urges? The solution is to replace them. You replace the impulse by finding other things in areas to focus on. You have to take those thoughts, as you deal with the biological rejection, and you have to find something more constructive and more positive to replace them with.

As in my years of counseling, I've found that an incarcerated environment is a great example of complete cutoff. They have zero access to their crutch, and so they find other things that fulfill that immediate vacancy. And this is what you have to start confronting and directing people to do, even if that means taking a hard look in the mirror at your own habits.

I want to tell you about a person I helped last year, someone that was court-ordered to go into a 28-day rehabilitation study. When the individual first came out, they were clean. The counselors had done their part and provided a foothold to rebuild self-esteem. Most importantly, the counselors provided the individual a method to create a similar environment, and move away from the toxic people in the individual's lives.

The problem was that the individual didn't have another environment to return to. They had burned all the other bridges in their lives, and the people they hurt were not yet ready to trust them or accept them back after 28 short days.

This is the worst possible outcome because they end up returning right back to the environment that first led to the breakdown. My patient ended up relapsing and failing the probationary period.

As a crisis counselor on the front lines, I always immediately let patients know that they're not the only ones who have taken a step backwards in their own personal recovery and growth.

You want to work on building up their esteem immediately. You want to let them know that it's human to err, and it's even worse to be judged for the error. Sometimes nothing more than simply offering them a moment's break – a chance to get away from that which they find themselves thrown right back into as a result of their ordeal based on prior life that has closed so many opportunities for them – helps them rebound and create new opportunities.

I've spent time as a chaplain in one of those environments. I chose to redirect people from that environment and meet with them somewhere familiar. I helped show them that there are creative options to escape any situation.

I encourage less contact with the people in that toxic environment you recently left, and instead tell them to find other people who can help you start transforming and processing your options.

With the right support structure, no matter how limited and dire the situation, you still have options that you can create. These must be done with love, compassion, and understanding, and non-judgmental affection.

Understand that these people are just other human beings that are genuinely scared and afraid, because they know they're afflicted, and they know that they are not yet at a personal stage where they can break free the chains of addiction.

From there, all you need is time and a goal. Even if it starts small. You need goals: measurable tasks that you can work towards and be successful doing. As you start seeing that success, the recovery can begin.

I can personally bear witness to people who are now clean for over 15 years as a result of that moment of compassion and understanding. You can create a safety zone anywhere. It's in the mind as to how you approach it.

CHAPTER SIX:
Communication

This chapter moves away from the physical and into your approach to the crisis. Communication, and the ability to successfully wield it, is paramount to emerging victorious in a crisis. The people you surround yourself with, and those you choose to communicate with during this time, will largely determine whether you succeed or fail. You must be disciplined about who you communicate with, and why.

Communication is essential for survival, and for being able to organize and coordinate your network of people. You may not have a working cell phone in a crisis. If so, then how do you connect with others? Sometimes you do it through a network of other people who are in the same situation you find yourself in. It's kind of like a relay race, during which runners pass a baton.

You need to communicate to someone on the other side of town, but due to the pandemic or due to some catastrophe, you're unable to connect with them electronically. Instead, think of a person who might help. If you know someone that may be heading in that direction, or you become introduced to somebody heading in that direction who can deliver the message, you can make contact using this intermediary.

I've been in foreign countries with extremely limited communication, and I have seen how people pass important information. You must creative, but you must also be selective. You must know the sources you trust. Picking the right person might mean the difference between life and death.

How do you trust an absolute stranger? How do you know who to make your ally? By taking advantage of neurolinguistics, the understanding and comprehension of how somebody receives the information you're trying to convey. You use their body language to determine whether or not this is a trustworthy resource. This is the essence of true effective communication.

Nonverbal Communication

People don't communicate with only their words. In fact, words convey only a small fraction of the true meaning. Studies have shown that as much as 70 percent of communication happens with our body, especially in scenarios of heightened stress. The best communicators take advantage of these nonverbal cues.

When confronting a stranger, ask yourself the following questions: How do they hold themselves, for instance? How engaged are their eyes? How is their posture? Are they shifting or tapping their feet? Are they drifting and looking at other things and becoming distracted?

These are very important physical features to analyze. This will help you spot someone deceptive or secretive. This is how to spot the truth.

Of course, in real life the person won't be looking away from you. Their giveaways will be much more subtle, like a small glance to the right before telling you a lie. Learning to identify these patterns of behavior can mean the difference between life and death.

It's vitally important to not only pay attention to their words and actions, but how they receive your words, in turn. Are they staying focused? Are they interested? Are they showing enthusiasm? Or are they showing a lack of attention, by turning away or looking around the room? You can tell how they're assessing the information you're giving to them by the way their body is responding to the information.

Say you initiate contact with someone you need to communicate through in order to get a message to a distant source. If this person is of a trusting nature, they're likely not going to sit with their arms folded, leaning backwards, halfway looking at you. They're going to be paying attention to anything you're trying to discuss with them, and that will come through clearly in their bodily actions.

A person you can trust, and with whom you can feel confident in conveying the information, would be sitting up in comfortably and in proper posture. They wouldn't have their arms locked in front of them. They would be open. They would be ideally focused and tuned into you and showing intent in the interest to hear what you have to say. The body language tells you if it is a type of person you can trust. "Steady" is a word I often use.

The opposite is so readily apparent. You can have someone looking directly at you, and they're not focused on you at all. They're shifty, unsettled, and shrink under pressure.

Tone is another aspect that becomes essential in effective communication. It is a kind of fusion between nonverbal and verbal, because it involves their words, but not only the words. Tone is about the inflection of their voice, the rise and fall of their pitch, and the emphasis on words and sounds that can help you determine their true motives. The tone of their voice can show that they are either trustworthy or untrustworthy.

As a rule, if the tone stays level and moderate in the conversation, you can assume that it is the truth. However, if you're in communication, and you recognize a drastic volume change, more stress in the voice, you may proceed with caution.

People with a truthful and honest nature stay relatively calm and direct when communicating. More often than not, anxiety and frustration mean someone has something to hide.

Inner Communication

The next side of communication is the inner dialogue. How you talk to yourself and interact with your own mind can be a source of great pain or great relief.

People, even kind, thoughtful people, can be extremely negative towards themselves. They are constantly putting themselves down in their own inner thoughts.

In a crisis, it is important that you monitor your inner communication. Your thoughts become your reality, and if you maintain a defeated mindset, your life outlook will reflect that.

Loneliness is a major problem in crisis. These moments can be the most isolated times of people's lives. They are likely without major resources and

Communication

community support. This makes loneliness another hurdle to overcome.

When loneliness grows within you, you start drifting into other thoughts. This is where negativity breeds. Instead of focusing on productive, concrete solutions, your mind focuses on the many negative factors that led to this situation. What people don't understand is: you have to train your mind. You need to train it to focus on the positive, and it will slowly begin to follow those patterns.

When you are alone in a hotel room, or completely isolated in some other environment, how do you evoke warmth in the room? Maybe it's as simple as opening the curtains to let the light in. Maybe you choose something as simple as turning on the TV. Perhaps you'll listen to music instead of watching the news.

Similarly, you can make choices in your immediate environment to remove or reduce the loneliness that starts to come upon you. You are compelled to change. If you don't change in that moment or transform in that moment, then you begin to slip towards depression. Your loneliness is amplified.

This is inner communication. It is occurring all the time within your own thoughts and your own mind. You want to channel your words and your thoughts in a positive direction, to be positive, to encourage yourself, and to be kind and gentle because you are going to get through this. You are going to turn this crisis into a victory. The more you encourage yourself and use positive words to lift yourself up, the faster and easier the road forward will be.

During my days as a hospice counselor, many times I sat in a room with a dying patient. Usually, this was someone without loved ones surrounding them. I would talk to them about the greatest memories with their mother, brother, or best friend, or a vacation they took to some foreign country – whatever it may be, as long as it was a positive memory. Eventually, inevitably, the body would begin the shutdown process. We were trained to look for these signs. When I knew they were close to death, I would always do the same thing.

I would get up next to their ear, and I would say, "Are you ready now?" I would start reminding them of all of the memories they had shared with me, and I would see their physical response to it. I could tell that their mind was drifting into these positive memories during perhaps the loneliest time in their life. Here they were, dying, no family or friends around them.

I know in my heart it made a world of difference. I could see it in their body as they drifted away. That is the power of communication – to lift anyone out of loneliness.

This book in itself can be a communication resource. Use it as a conversation starter. Hand it to somebody who is in your immediate environment or somebody you want to connect with in order to have this conversation. The more people in your communication network, the more powerful your victory will be.

Share this book and communicate with others about what you are learning. Encourage them to confront their own crises.

CHAPTER SEVEN:
Unlocking Meditation

Let's start with an exercise I personally use every single day. I am advocating for two meditation pauses, no more than 15 minutes apiece, in the morning and again before bed. These moments of reflection and centering are of major benefit to anyone who is experiencing elevated levels of stress – and during a crisis, your stress may be at an all-time high.

Meditation is a powerful relaxer, and allows you to calm the mind, body, and soul, and bring the self to unity. In doing so, you cleanse your thoughts of any negative ideas and perspectives. You bring clarity to your thoughts, which translates to improved action.

When done correctly, meditation and breathing exercises prepare your mentality for any challenge. They improve focus, elevate mood, and might be perhaps the most important things you can do for your body that require no outside assistance or resources.

Most days, and especially during a crisis, you cannot afford to be distracted. You cannot afford to waste precious time and energy on factors outside of your control. Meditation allows you to focus solely on survival and strip everything else away. Any non-essential thoughts and feelings are let go completely. They are separate from your larger goals.

This is the power of meditation. It gives you the tools to channel your intention into a single drive, to push everything else to the side. When this happens, you're practically unstoppable. You don't see obstacles anymore – you only see your goals.

Meditation and Me

Meditation was introduced to me at the University of Sedona when I was a student there. I was working on my master's degree, and free meditation trials were offered for students to improve academic performance.

Meditation was one of my areas of study at the time. Once I learned the power of true meditation, I never stopped practicing. I still do two sessions every day, and I recommend you try something similar. I only encourage it because I have seen firsthand the incredible impact meditation offers.

Many days, people wake up and already feel overwhelmed. They are still locked in the experiences and troubles of the day before. Or, they are lying awake at night, trying to still their mind enough to drift into sleep.

This is where meditation becomes so important. The techniques are simple, and if you type "Meditation Practice" into any search engine you'll find hundreds of resources. The central idea is always the same. The most important factor is that you are actively calming the mind, calming the body, and calming the soul. Focus on one principle thought, and eliminate any intruding thoughts that may be competing by refocusing back to that thought.

For me, I focus on my breathing, and push everything else away. That becomes my focal point. Your mind becomes empty, and you become aware of all the sensations in your body.

Learning and using these techniques has dramatically improved my own focus and quality of life. In the morning, using meditation has taught me how to focus on my objective for the day, and nothing else. I am not looking a day or two down the road. My only intention is to find success in my single set of daily tasks. In the evenings, I use those 20 minutes to review, reset, and regenerate my energy for the next day. It allows me to start fresh every night, so to speak.

The most beautiful thing about meditation is how little time it truly takes, and how dramatically it can improve your quality of life in as little as 30 minutes a day.

If I told the average person, "I have a way to make you happier, healthier, less stressed, more focused, and improve your waking experience in less than 30 minutes a day," most would think I am trying to scam them. But meditation really does all that.

There are a number of concrete scientific studies that have proven the effectiveness of meditation in improving quality of life. The biggest hindrance is a lack of commitment. Meditation is hard work. It may sound easy to sit quietly with your eyes closed, but that misses the essence of the practice. You need to be willing to push back on your own thoughts and focus your energy on a single point. This takes time and patience, but, like anything, it gets easier with practice.

Once a person starts the process of accepting a few moments of calmness, solitude and focusing on a singular thought, it becomes very easy. It becomes second nature to slip into a meditative state.

Meditation is ideal for anyone in crisis mode. When your entire life has been totally and completely upended, you must regroup within yourself. You are the greatest tool at your disposal. You are your own best asset. In order to be your most successful, you must have clarity and preparation. Meditation gives you both.

If the entire world meditated, and I fully believe this to be true, it would be a much happier and more fulfilling place to live. People would focus on the important things in life, and they could wake up in the morning with a renewed sense of purpose each day.

Sometimes when you, yourself, don't have a sense of what your direction should be, meditation can help you find it. When you rid yourself of the mental noise, the only thoughts left are your pure intentions and ideas – undiluted and ready to be realized.

A Path to Salvation

I've seen meditation help solve even deep-rooted addictions. A few years ago, I was working with a methamphetamine addict. Every decision he made and every single action he took were in the pursuit of his drug habit. His world was crashing down around him. He finally decided that he no longer wanted to pursue a life that was totally and completely catastrophic.

Over the course of perhaps nine months of counseling, we were able to transform him into a successful and valuable member of his community. He moved on to become a counselor.

During our time together, he learned through meditation about calming, recreating, and rebuilding himself – through himself. That's the key, right there. We are the vessel of our own salvation, but we have to still the storm that encompasses our life, and we have to find a resource. What better resource than the self?

When I recommend daily meditation to patients and friends, a common reply sounds something like this: "Twice a day? How do you expect me to fit all that in?"

I understand it may appear daunting at first, but I assure you each day gets easier. And I often point out in response that smoking a cigarette or drinking a cup of coffee takes about the same amount of time. But those can be detrimental. Meditation is only beneficial.

If you want to make time, you'll be able to. Oftentimes it is as simple as your willingness to commit. Start your evening routine a little earlier, and give yourself that morning cushion to sit quietly at the table. These small acts may feel like concessions or a waste of time, but they will dramatically change your experience if done correctly. In that sense, they may be the most important part of your day.

Meditation also brings joy, which is an underestimated way to stay afloat during a crisis. Without joy in your life, you are robbing life itself of the beautiful gift that is pure happiness.

In my old life, I used to wake up thinking about what obstacles I had to overcome in my criminal world, what I had to do to stay alive, and if I would go to jail today for the rest of my life. I had to wake up with those kinds of thoughts, and the burden of that affected my mind and my health.

When I finally started using meditation in the morning many years later, it was like a complete life shift. I could focus on the parts of life that brought me joy.

As a result, my life became enriched and full, and I replaced anger and hostile instincts with something that was beautiful and peaceful and calm. People identified my transition, and all of a sudden those around me started wanting what I was showing them.

We set and lead by example in this life. The joy of seeing other people resurfacing from their own conflicts and finding peace and joy is a truly uplifting feeling, and it spreads like a virus. It's an amazing thing. In the process, I felt like meditation was guiding me and showing me how to become aligned within myself.

This meditation was ultimately born out of my faith in God and Christianity. All of my life I was a Christian, but it wasn't until I went to prison that I could accept Christianity, and take the time to complete my studies to get to where I knew that I was being led.

While I'd always been a believer, I was never in an opportunity where I could calm my life, still in my life, and prepare my life to receive the necessary tools to represent and glorify God and give thanks for the life He gave me. It came in that moment.

I remember the first time I gave a sermon. I was in a cell and I fell to my knees, unable to take the burden of the criminal life any longer. As I mentioned earlier, God sent two people in, one to be on each side of me. As each one of them came in the door, they embraced my shoulders with love and care and compassion. In that moment all of the chains broke. All of the anger and all of the hatred and all of the violence left me completely. I was transformed. I was able to give the sermon to the men at my side, both of whom were already born-again Christians.

Prison afforded me the time necessary to pursue a goal that my spirit needed to fulfill. I utilized every minute. From the moment I woke up until the minute I went to sleep at night, I was in constant study. I was continually learning that which would benefit others down the road. I knew I could take these life experiences and make sense of them and expand upon them for the goodness of all.

Crisis Victory

One of my darkest periods led to my salvation, as so often is the case. I found both God and the value of meditation behind those bars.

# CHAPTER EIGHT: Moving into the New

This chapter puts in place all the pieces you have gathered. It is about being prepared to move into the new phase of your post-crisis life.

After following every step laid out for you in this book, you should now have the tools to build a new and better life. You are ready to build a community and move into your newly transformed situation.

Now that you have accomplished acceptance, take this confidence, take these tools and the abilities to know how to properly use these tools, and start the rebuilding process. You have accomplished every goal set to this point and used the wisdom of the prior chapters to form the person you have become.

You are now ready to thrive. You have acquired a location. You have acquired resources to take care of all of your personal, immediate needs. You have acquired forms of communication, networking with other like-minded people – those who may or may not be going through the same type of crisis, but approach life in the same way.

Now that you have gathered everything and brought it all together, you are now ready to put yourself back into the community. Here, the goal is to be influential to others and aid and assist in their growth and their progression. This in turn benefits you, as it strengthens your connection to the environment.

Helping other like-minded individuals who are going through the same type of crisis you may be exiting is a way to build and solidify your network. Remember, humans by nature are wired to need social stimulation. Humans do not exist by themselves. You need to be uniformly attached to your community, and you need a comfortable setting in order to grow and self-cultivate.

Now that you've survived the initial fallout of the crisis, you can pivot to building and sharpening the tools you've acquired. These tools are meant to help build a fulfilling life, one that is pleasant, and based on new circumstances and changes. You need to find other people that have the same goal set that you have. Don't sacrifice on this point. Do not settle for anything less than what you know you fully deserve. It has to be as if you were entering into a marriage, where both people need to be equally yoked.

Both you and the community you build need to be on the same path, with the same goal and the same direction. That way, there's no friction. You have survived the friction, survived the immediate crisis, and now you are acquiring these people to build a community. A successful community is one where people have different strengths and weaknesses, but they all work in harmony to make it a successful entity. You have people who are gatherers. You have people who are counselors and meditators. You have people who are food preparers and shelter builders. Each person brings a gift, their talent, into the colonization concept that you find yourself designing, creating, and bringing together for mutual salvation.

This viewpoint dictates that all humans are needed. There are roles to be filled by every person, regardless of what each has been through, or the choices they've made. A community needs each member to be actively contributing and participating. It gives purpose to all involved.

Humans are not designed in nature to do it all alone. But before you catapult yourself into some community, you must have the necessary tools to be not only secure and protected but beneficial to the growth of the community. Everyone who separates themselves and tries to survive a crisis fails unequivocally. They get taken out. They either end up with illness or they end up with a lack of the necessary provisions to sustain a quality life. You can't survive on your own. You must have a team.

The team provides positive affirmations. Every day you participate, your value is reinforced. Everyone wants to feel needed. It strengthens your sense of self, as well as the ties of the community around you. This in turn bolsters your ability to actively participate and contribute. It becomes a kind of snowball of good intention and positive response. This is a healthy way to live. It is the ideal way to live.

Adding to our earlier chapter, meditation is a great way to build on these positives. By focusing in the morning for a few minutes you can see your progression. You feel the increasing benefit of stilling the mind and calming the soul. You focus on a singular thought. You have a goal set for the day, and you have the mindset to see it through. This helps you see the larger picture and gives each day a sense of importance.

You are able to achieve so much more when focusing your attention on one point. It is the distraction and the jumping in and out of different thought patterns that waste the most time. It limits your capacity and your energy.

Humans by nature must feel valued. They must feel that they matter to the whole; otherwise, their own path becomes a confusing disarray, and with that comes a lack of desire to complete tasks successfully.

In a crisis, maintaining calm is crucial. You have to be able to put yourself in a mindset that is not only beneficial to your personal survival, but to the environment.

Let me return to the example of cartel's kill order on me. As I detailed, just a few months before I wrote this book, they executed the order.

As the hitman repeatedly stabbed me, I felt my life leaving me. I reached a point of acceptance. Though I took steps to ensure the best chance of survival, the moment I accepted the likelihood of my death, I felt a wave of peace and calmness unlike any I had experienced. This serenity was in stark contrast to the years I spent in a hostile environment where violence and killings were commonplace.

When acceptance was reached, the struggle of life as I knew it was over.

When I awoke, I remember feeling conflicted, wondering why I was back here. I couldn't find an answer for it. I was upset that I had just left such a peaceful place.

It is so odd – knowing that you are dead, and all of a sudden you find yourself alive. It is literally unexplainable. It's an experience that you can only understand if you've lived it and come out the other side.

Be that as it may, a purpose was revealed to me shortly after. I realized that my life was restored so that I could work for God. My role, I learned, was to serve God and thus realize a purpose started 30 years ago when I gave my life to Him.

Once that became clear to me, I've become able to accept why I am still here. Every day I thank God for the life that He returned me to. It is truly an opportunity I do not plan to waste.

It not only makes me appreciate day-to-day life in a whole new way, but it makes me seek out the reasons why I was given another chance at life.

What is my purpose right now? I think it is to expand on the knowledge, the skills, and the experience that I have survived throughout the decades of coming from sin to redemption. This transformation is part of the cleansing process for me. It was like being born again, yet again. I am now on a day-to-day journey, sharing not only the testimony of a near-death experience, but the purpose of being brought back.

I realize my purpose is to aid and assist people who are struggling with crises. I want them to understand that a deeper love, compassion, peace, and calmness come with the acceptance of a situation we can't change. Through the challenge, we obtain greater wisdom and understanding.

As a hospice counselor, I watched dozens of people going through the dying process. Now, I understand that peace I would see in their eyes as they said their final "I love you" or "God bless you" as they passed into eternity. I understand now. I've been there. I've said that goodbye.

After trauma, life can feel empty. The path forward can be murky. The purpose for living may not be apparent. You must seek purpose, one that will benefit God, society, and self. You have to listen to that calmer voice.

Since the beginning of the book, one key point has been, what is your greatest asset? Your greatest asset is you, yourself. But determining your actual purpose is a challenge to discover independently. The best way to discover it is by leaning on a higher authority. In my case it was God, through Jesus. The important thing is to know that you cannot wrestle through it alone.

You must have a guiding point that you can find internally, and this will direct your purpose. It will take you down that path that gives glorification to the universe, not to just self. You're only a component in all of this. You're just a segment. Once you accept that, then purpose becomes revealed to us.

Bear in mind that your purpose won't materialize on your schedule. It has to be revealed. You can work on self-improvement and self-settlement as you are waiting for the purpose to become revealed to you.

I'm at this point as I wake up every single day wondering why the hell I came back to this mess when I had found ultimate peace. It's amazing! It is becoming revealed to me that this book is a purpose. I am here to reach out and help somebody.

Forgiveness After Suffering

Another important aspect in the aftermath of a crisis is forgiveness. Once you have re-stabilized your life, you may find that you are actually in a better and more courageous place as a result of perseverance. You've succeeded.

You may have a new foundation and a new personal way of expressing, contributing and knowing yourself. But you may also be experiencing residual trauma or anger towards another person or community. Despite finding success, any wrongdoing may still linger in your mind. This, in turn, adds stress.

If you're experiencing this, hopefully by this point in our journey you've begun to understand the removal of guilt and its importance. But understand this: Forgiveness is momentary. What is more important than forgiveness is acceptance of your new life change. Forgiveness will become a pattern, part of that life change and that experience. Guilt will already be accepted and understood by the person who is carrying the guilt. The same is true for anger and hate – and any other negative emotion that needs to be let go.

As I indicated, during my moment of transformation, my moment of true-life conversion, all of my negativity gave way to that which was greater than me. At that moment, I felt it pulling the anger and pain out of me. All that was left was truth.

I hope to help you ascend to the point of forgiveness, acknowledging the removal of anger, hatred, and betrayal, and any other limiting feelings spurred by the crisis.

Today, I actually love the man who stabbed me. I hold no bitterness of any kind for him. I didn't even have negative thoughts when he was trying to kill me. It was amazing, because it was proof of the truth that I speak and preach to people every day. He was taking my life and I loved him anyway. I really truly did.

I've taken down high-level criminals where I've laid a hand on their shoulder and prayed for them, and watched them break and cry and say, "Thank God it's over."

I've known assassins who couldn't forgive themselves, and through prayer and passing it onto a greater power I have seen them lift up their guilt and get rid of their self-anger and hatred for what they did. I've seen them cast it away with my own eyes.

You get there only through acceptance. You have to accept that which you've created. People are not born killers and assassins, and they're not born drug smugglers. You choose that through circumstances that befall us in life, and when you hit a crossroads you take the wrong turn in an impulsive moment.

Once you accept that some of the turns led to our crisis or catastrophe, the rebirth can begin.

The main idea in this entire book is acceptance. Once you accept what you were, you can recreate what you become. Believe me, I'm a living example of that.

Thirty years ago, you would not have liked the man I was. I didn't even like the man I was. Back then, I had no remorse for any action I took towards another human being. Back then, nothing came above my own survival. I turned off or repressed any vulnerable feelings.

Acceptance shows us how to turn the feelings back on, and to rise above those experiences in our life, to become something worthy to contribute to this beautiful universe. Once that awareness comes within us and you accept the awareness of this newly transformed person that you are, then great things can happen – not just for yourself, but for everyone around you.

If you continue to carry anger, all you do is rob yourself of that daily joy and you remove glory from God, your creator. You cannot walk with anger, oppression, or any other type of a negative conceptual feeling. If you're carrying that stuff, it will destroy you.

Most importantly, it's not about self and ego, which destroy those around you who love you and care for you, and who are influenced by your daily exposure to their life.

Forgiveness really is the path to freedom. You have to forgive yourself. I stand today as living proof that you can forgive. Freedom is on the other side.

Do not allow yourself to wake up in the morning with a negative thought. If it pursues you, it will create a negative day. You must wake up and remove negativity as immediately as possible, and then replace it with kindness, compassion, love and care for other people.

If you end up frustrated and you're dealing with frustration, the best way to break the cycle of frustration is the reprocessing of your morning thought when you start your day. Frustration will self-eliminate given time and attention.

Anxiety is another battle for a lot of people. The way you remove your anxiety is to calm the mind and focus on one single entity. What are you going to accomplish today, and what do you need to get to that accomplishment? This helps to remove other negative thoughts or impulses that come into your life that will set the direction of the day ahead.

Additionally, goal-setting initiatives are vital to survival. You must have a goal set every morning of your day. It can be a giant one or a small one. But it has to be a real one that you know you can accomplish. It gives purpose, and that purpose defines your path ahead. These teachings all come in the pursuit of acceptance and success.

The Long Goodbye

This is the end of our journey together. Thank you for following this path with me and working to improve.

It is my sincerest hope that you follow the guidelines in this book. I can assure you, through my own experiences of coming from sin to redemption, that you will find joy, calm, and love on the other side. If you are able to embrace these teachings, the rest of your days will be filled with an unspeakable joy that you never even knew existed.

Sometimes it takes a crisis to yield these moments, when you realize exactly how critical it is to glorify each day by waking up in that compassion, joy, and love.

The purpose of this book is to aid people who find themselves in a crisis. My hope is that it has equipped you to weather personal crises as a better, more well-rounded person. I want you to realize the joy, comfort, and compassion that each day offers you.

My personal journey into and out of crisis started when I was 15 years old. It is still with me 51 years later. You've heard my perils, and you've listened to my high points. And through all of it, I still found victory.

I know you can do the same. The path is laid out for you now, should you choose to take it. The pieces to find success are in front of you, now it is up to you how you move forward with them.

We've set up a community that I invite you to explore at the website www.crisisvictory.com. Please visit if you'd be interest in reading more stories of people overcoming enormous odds. I invite you to consider joining the community, connecting with others who are also on this mission, and perhaps contributing your own story. Who knows? It may be the inspiration someone else needs.

Best of luck in everything that lies ahead. Thank you.

A CHANGED LIFE:
From Crisis to Victory

His son, Alex, is Pastor Hal's pride and joy.

His love of motorcycles helps this pastor break out of stereotypical barriers.

Forgiveness is the path to freedom. You have to forgive yourself.
PASTOR HAL

Pastor Hal and his nephew are both proud veterans.

Pat Grady, left, was instrumental in developing Pastor Hal's cocaine empire. He was sentenced to 36 years and was released after serving 22 years. Today, they have cleaned up their lives and remain steadfast friends.

From Crisis to Victory

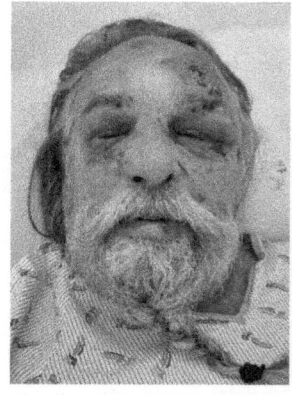

On June 7, 2020, Pastor Hal survived a cartel kill order.

Pastor Hal, right, spends time with a hospice patient who died in fall 2019.

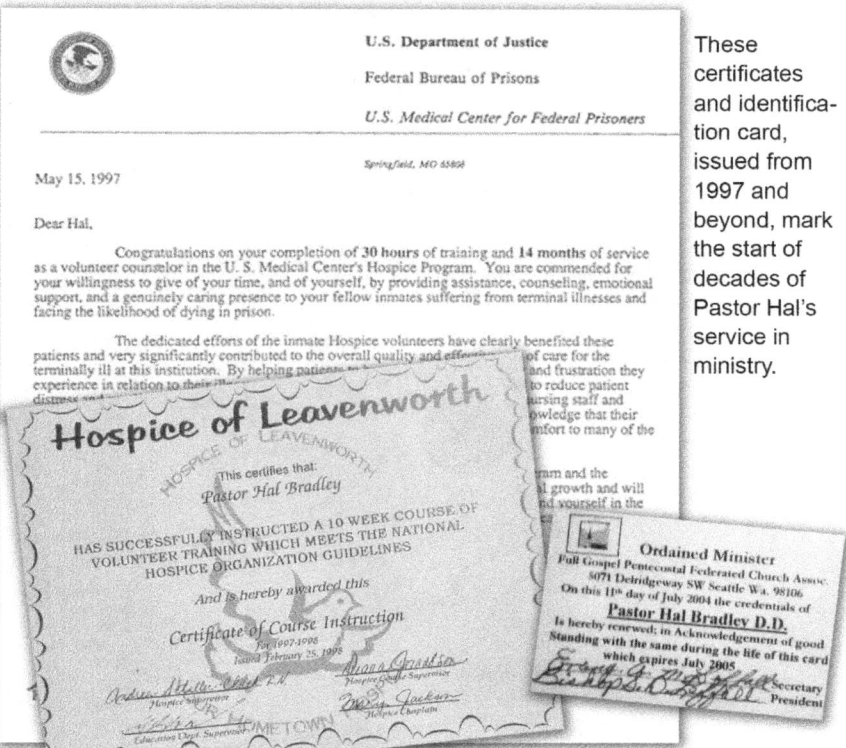

These certificates and identification card, issued from 1997 and beyond, mark the start of decades of Pastor Hal's service in ministry.

www.ingramcontent.com/pod-product-compliance
Lightning Source LLC
LaVergne TN
LVHW011425080426
835512LV00005B/263